T0090822

The Time Has Come For Mankind to Know the Truth

You Will Not Die

From a Missing Link in Today's Educational Format

The only link that can establish

unity, peace, prosperity and happiness

of the body of mankind.

By

D R . M . M . S R E E N I V A S A N

With A Chapter On The Greatest Tragedy;
The Meaning Of September 11, 2001

Order this book online at www.trafford.com
or email orders@trafford.com

Most Trafford titles are also available at major online book retailers.

Printed in the United States of America.

ISBN: 978-1-4269-4776-6 (sc)
ISBN: 978-1-4269-4777-3 (e)

Trafford rev. 01/12/2011

www.trafford.com

North America & International
toll-free: 1 888 232 4444 (USA & Canada)
phone: 250 383 6864 ♦ fax: 812 355 4082

Prologue

"Death" and"Dying" spells finality in the minds of many. The mystery behind such an event that will inevitably happen in the life of every human being is the cause of fear that creates a sense of hopelessness in the minds of many.

If "Death" and "Dying" can cause fear, the fact that "You Will Not Die" will cause even greater fear. Many are not aware of this fact. The reason to share the contents of this book is to cause the reader to escape the inevitable result "eternal remorse" due to sheer ignorance of the true meaning behind these words; "You Will Not Die"!

This book will attempt to impress in the minds of every reader that what any human being should fear most is not the knowledge that "death" is finality. On the other hand, what they must fear most is when they know for a truth that a part of any human being; that which is real and immortal will not die.

Why should a human being fear most when one realizes that one will not die? When a human being comes to realize that "death" is not the end of life and living and that this immortal part which will continue to live is not equipped with what it will require before one leaves this human world upon "death"; this realization will cause fear.

The truth is that if that immortal part of a human being is not equipped with what it will require to be attracted to and to live eternally in joy, life in this human world on planet earth is futile!

This book attempts to share this most important and fundamental truth in a way that the reader will find it easy to understand. The reason for this sharing is because of a love relationship between the author and any human being on earth who in the mind of the author is a dear member of one human family!

There are places in the script of this book when certain facts are repeated. This is to cause a deeper imprint in the mind of the reader so that right facts will fall into right slots to solve a puzzle or a picture in the mind. There are also certain places in the script when the author without mincing words state some facts openly and directly, which might cause the reader to question the authority of the author to make such statements; This is also a feeling that arises from this love-relationship. For example if the reader comes across a shade of one's understanding about the fact where it is written; *"No one can reach and live a joyous eternal life if the facts revealed in this book is not understood and lived"* the author reserves the right to apologize for making such comments and upsetting the reader, but as you read this book again and again you will know that what has been stated in this book is pure Truth!

Read this book with an open mind!

A Special Note to The Reader

Congratulations dear reader for having chosen to read this book.

The contents of this book "You Will Not Die", is a very special knowledge. It can be referred to as a "missing link" in today's education. The unearthing of this knowledge is a result of more than four decades of search, study, research and ultimate understanding. This is a subject the generality of the people of the world are not interested in or keen to know. This attitude and choice happens to be a mistake! Mankind in this day is paying dearly for that mistake. This most important knowledge is now offered to every human being on planet earth. Only when they choose to study, understand and act upon what this book offers, will they end up living a worthwhile and a purposeful life. On the contrary should they wish not to know and understand what this book offers, assuredly they will be living a life that will end in eternal remorse. This is a fact!

In order to really grasp the Truth which this book reveals it is necessary for the reader to read this book not once but many times. This loving advice is given solely for the sake of you, the reader! The reader must make every attempt to understand the most important knowledge which make up the contents of this book!. When the reader understands that which is explained between the covers of this book, that fortunate reader will enter a new and an exciting new dimension of understanding to know the purpose of human existence. This knowledge will in turn before it is too late, when transformed into right deeds will cause a mindset change, and this will be followed by wanting to live purpose-fulfilling lifestyles!

The message within the covers of this book is a powerful knowledge that can be a true-life-giving and true-life-changing message.

It is only when you understand even a glimpse of what the message within the covers of this book conveys to your heart will you appreciate the priceless quality of love that had energized and drove a mission to deliver truth to reach the heart of every human being in this day.

May you be blessed and empowered when you in turn become a source of guidance to all who populate planet earth!

The Author

Forward

Exploring every opportunity comes with a beginning. Your opportunity to independently investigate Truth has a beginning too. Now is the time when the opportunity for those who have chosen to live a knowledge-rich, purposeful-life has arrived. Begin right now. It is destined. That is why you have chosen to read this book.

It is not premature to declare right now, that, before you leave this world; before you end your journey in this world, had you not come across this book, you assuredly would have been a victim of eternal remorse! It is not premature to declare right now, that, had you come across this book and chose not to seriously try to understand the contents therein, the result will be that your journey in this life on planet earth as a human being in this human dimension, in the end you will assuredly face eternal remorse! Yes, eternal remorse!

Be happy therefore that amongst the billions of people out there you now have an opportunity to know truth-laden answers to the following questions that have baffled and confused mankind through the ages!. Questions like; "Who am I?", "Why am I created a human being?", "Where have I come from?", "Why am I travelling from birth to death in this human dimension?", "I am also travelling through time, space, knowledge, etc. and again why?", "If I am a traveler and if I do not know who I am and where I am going to, how can this life be purposeful?, "Is there a heaven and hell?", etc. etc.

This book will, with uncanny clarity, share with you answers to all questions you wanted answered truthfully! Written as a result of being divinely inspired by the "Light of Truth", you are assured of receiving the right knowledge of what you should know while living as a human being!

Think of your past times! At some period in your life you have searched to know the truth about the reality of living a life as a human being and you have believed in answers that you have come across from many sources. These answers; did they reflect Truth? If it was not from the "Light" of Truth", will it not be wise to know what is right and what is wrong, before it is too late? If you were living a life believing in Truth, and find out that you were truly living a life based on false beliefs and vain imaginations, will you not want to know how to live the remaining days of your life purposefully? If mankind had lived according to what is right, why then has the body of mankind in this day become sick and riddled with all types of wayward diseases and has reached the sorry state it is in now! Think!

Think! For many thousands of years, mankind has been living lives driven by superstition, vain imaginings and idle fancies! This state of affairs within the body of mankind has resulted in great and greater suffering of the peoples everywhere. Not a day passes when news items bring to the attention of people around the world about humans who kill humans, plunder, rape, steal, torture, and live lives worse than wild animals! All these are perpetrated by human beings who have been created within the mould of love and noble qualities! Are we not a part of living within this miserable scenario? Is there a solution? When you understand the Truth as revealed in this book you will know that there is a solution! You will also know that you are also a part of this solution!

Knowledge must be followed by a willingness to want to, in deeds materialize through transformation, such knowledge in our lives. Just as knowledge alone is not enough and wanting to transform this knowledge in this life is also not enough; the Truth is to transform this knowledge into deeds! The knowledge that you will come to know after understanding the contents in this book will bring about a change; a change that will contribute towards making this world a better world! Only then will you be able to experience the beauty of living as a true and noble human being! Is this not what any human being should aspire to become?

The following one of the many examples will illustrate the extent of the shroud of ignorance that has blinded people from knowing the truth about human existence.

Allow me to ask you this question: *"Given a choice and if indeed you want to come back to live once again as a human being, will you want to come back again to live in the kind of human-world that is prevalent now on planet earth? Or will you want to come back to live in a far, far better world?"*.

For sure your answer will be; *"This world? Come back to live another life in this rotten world? Oh no! Who will ever want to live in this unhappy world? I will never want to come back to this cruel world? No Sir, Not this world! Perhaps a better world!"*

Allow me to ask you another question: *"Do you love your children?"*

I know what any parent will answer. They will say loud and clear with great emphasis and feeling: *"Which parent will not love their children? Of course I love my children."*

This is what I will tell them: *"If you say with so much passion and feelings that you really love your children, then why did you "invite" them to come to this world; a world you abhor so much; a world you know is not fit for our children to be nurtured to grow up as noble human beings!"*

Our children did not have a choice! Soon they will know that it was their parents who were responsible to "invite" them to come into this world. It is only later on in life when it is too late will they realize the folly of their parents who were not equipped with the knowledge as to what is the meaning of Marriage and Family! In the end many do not even realize when they themselves will become as wicked and wanton as their fellow peers!

In this context, do you really love your children?

I have tried many a time to ask such questions and I have always received a reply like this: *"Please let us know what we can do about it."*

"Please advise us!"

"Now that as you say, we have invited our children into this dirty world, what can we do about it?"

Dear reader. If you are an adult know this fact; that this human world is not yours to possess. You are not an owner of this human world. You are only a builder. You are building a world for the next generation. You are building a world with what technology you have at this time! The technology that you possess at this time, is far, far advanced than before times! Don't you think it futile to use, outworn for this life in this day, older technologies? Let us reason! Let us wake up!

The world we adults now live in truly belongs to our children and future generations. They are the ones who will inherit this world. What type of world are you giving them as a gift? This kind of rotting world? How sad to realize that children and future generations who will arrive to populate this world will realize and know what a bad, bad world they have been invited to arrive and inherit! It is practically disgusting when we come to realize the type of gift our children and unborn generations of the future will inherit! Yet we claim that we love our children!

The most painful part of this scenario is the fact that when we leave this human world at the end of our journey here, we will know what a dirty world we have left behind for our children to inherit. At that time finding ourselves impotent because there is nothing we can do from where we have gone to, and knowing that there is no way to rectify our mistakes; this too will contribute to our living an eternity of eternal remorse!

When are we going to realize the fact that through ignorance we have built a world which is wicked to the core? When are we going to realize that we; every human being will have to change the lifestyles we live in now, in order to change this human world so that it can become a far, far better world, which we can offer to our children and future generations as a gift to inherit?

When? Have we any options? One future day we will leave this world. How long will it take for this future to come upon us! When we will arrive, or be born into this human-world and when we are destined to leave this human-world is not a choice in the hands of any human being! We have an X number of years to live and as the seconds tick away, the duration of our existence in this human-world becomes less and less. This is the truth! When do we start to begin to contribute our share of goodness to make this human world a world of unity, peace, prosperity and happiness? Will we be proud of gifting to our children and unborn future generations the likes of the world we now live in?

When? When shall we start to change this human world? The time is now! Why? Because, the horrible, unbelievable happenings committed by human beings in this day, is escalating every moment. The body of mankind is under siege by worse-than-animal behavior patterns that are draining its vitality and causing vast damage to its existence! All these happenings have come about because of ignorance; an ignorance about the purpose for which every human being is created to live in this human dimension for an X number of years!

When you read and understand what this book attempts to convey to your heart, you will then arrive at a realization that not only you and every human being has been created by an Almighty Creator, but you have also been given the power and capacity to plan your life in such a way as to make it possible for you to contribute your share to make this world a far, far better world; a heaven on earth!!

You might not have known about this truth until now! Never mind. Where there is life there is hope! When you come to know and understand the Truth as you finish reading and understanding this message of love, you will come to realize how you as a human being has been destined to become a change-agent to build a world that will reflect in thoughts, words and deeds, the attributes of a Loving Creator!

When you bask under the light of Truth which you will discover through your independent investigation about you, mankind, and the Creator of all, you will be so thankful that you decided to read this book!

May your efforts to search for Truth to know who you are and for what purpose you have been created a human being cause you to transform yourself; your lifestyle and allow this change to contribute to effect a change of the body of humankind you are part of!

Chapter 1

<u>Who Am I?</u>

Let us start reading this book by you asking yourself, "Who am I?"

Do you know who you are? How many out there know who we human beings are? We find that in all Holy Books of the past and the present, it is revealed, *"Know thy self"* So it is a very important step to take when we wish to independently investigate Truth. We have to heed this advice and search to know about oneself!

If you do not know who you are and why you were created to live a certain number of years as a human being in this human dimension on planet earth, whatever you do in this life will be a wasted effort. Every effort you make to fulfill desires that contribute to living a material life will be a wasted effort!

You are a traveler in this life. You travel every moment through time and space, through knowledge and experience. We all know that when we are born into this world; when we enter this world from the world of our mother's womb, we begin our journey in this world from the point of birth and will end our journey one day in the future. If you do not know who you are and why you are travelling you may end your journey to reach a place you did not want to be. What then? Can you retrace your journey to make corrections to once again reach where you wish to be? Impossible! There is no return back into this human dimension as a human being. In this world of time and space there is no going back! This is Truth!

If you do not travel according to a plan, the destination you reach can be a forbidden place you abhor and what happens is that you will in the end reach that abhorrent place and conditions surrounding it and continue to live there through eternity! This is what is meant by ending up to live in "eternal remorse

Surely you do not want to experience such an eternity! Surely you will want to know the right pathway to travel while still living in this human dimension in order to reach where you will enjoy a life of wonder and beauty through eternity! How can you achieve your desire? By reading and understanding the special knowledge prescribed in this book, and to continue after that to independently investigate to know more about Truth! Then and only then will you begin and to want to live a lifestyle conducive to attracting the love and guidance of the Almighty Creator! Will a Creator who created us with so much love abandon us? Ours the duty to cry out and beg guidance from the Almighty Creator to guide us to walk the right Highway of Life, back to Him in Paradise!

How is it possible to make us; you, I and all human beings understand that unwittingly we might end our journey in this life to reach to live an eternal life in Hellish conditions? We must therefore know how to walk the right Highway of Life to reach Heavenly conditions! Therefore "To Know" is important! It is possible! This book will share with you as to how! One of the reasons why it is possible is because we as human beings are created with a gift of power, capacity to know and also with the power of choice; to choose the right from the wrong! Can there be any doubt that many have abused this privilege?

Everything in this world has been created by an Almighty Creator. To nothing He has created, has He given the power of choice. The power of choice is given to only human beings. Know this fact! It is Truth! Only human beings have the power to either obey or disobey the Laws of God. The reason for how terrible the body of mankind has sunk into is because of willful ignorance, due to wrong choice-making on the part of human beings and who do not know nor wish to know the answer to the question. "Who am I?"

If you are able to answer the following questions based on Truth, you can be sure that you are travelling every moment on the right pathway to where you want to go when your journey in this life ends!

Who am I?

How do I look like?

For what purpose am I travelling in this human dimension on planet earth?

As a traveler in this human dimension, where am I going to?

How can I know how to choose the right road to where I am going to?

If I had in ignorance travelled the wrong road until now, how can I know how to change directions and travel along the right road?

When will I know that I am travelling the wrong road so that I can decide to choose to travel hence-forwards, the right road?

Out of these seven questions if you can answer based on Truth, just two questions, consider yourself very fortunate. This means that you can read and understand the contents of this book and in deeds you can tailor to live a life of joy and happiness, peace and harmony with you and your family and with all of mankind! You will also be very happy to have gained such a precious knowledge, before the end of your journey in this human world!

If you are not able to answer any of the questions based on Truth, you are truly living a purposeless life which will take you to reach a destination that will cause you eternal remorse! Immediately make up your mind to read and understand the contents of this book before it is too late! Be serious to follow up on your choice and decision! No one can foretell when one's journey of life in this human dimension in this material world will come to an end!

This book therefore will be an apt primer to lead you to know Truth and thence forward you will have to make a decision and choose to independently investigate Truth and in deeds dictated by such knowledge live by what you know is guidance from the "Light" of Truth"!

Why independently investigate? It is because every human being in this day has been given the power to choose to know the answers to all these questions. Not only has a human being given the mighty power to choose to do what one wants, but also the power and capacity to independently investigate to know what is right and what is wrong!

Therefore as you read to understand the contents of this book, with faith and belief in the powers you are created with potentially, assure yourself that you can release this power and capacity to understand all that is written herein and that you also have the power and capacity to transform what you know into deeds!

Chapter 2

<u>Who are you?</u>

You are now reading this book. You are now looking at the words on this page?

Are your eyes looking at the words on this page? What will be your answer, Yes or No?

If you answer is, "Yes" you are wrong. If you answer "No" then who is looking at the words on this page? The right answer is "I" am looking at the words on this page!

Then who is the "I"? Who is the "I" that is looking at this page?" Who is the "I" that is reading this book?

Know this, that your eyes are not looking at the words on this page, but YOU, (You call yourself "I"); you are using your eyes as a tool to look at this page.

Can you understand this simple explanation about the "You", the "I"?

"You" are an invisible entity. "You" are real! "You", "Me" and "I" are that same invisible entity.

You are known by many names, like soul, atma, lingwan etc. Let us stick to the word "soul" to describe the "I", the "Me" and "You"

In Truth, you are right when you declare, *"I am reading the words on this page using my eyes as a tool." "I am holding this book using my hands as a tool.", "I am walking using my legs as tools", and "I am touching this table using my arm and my finger which are tools"*

In Truth, a human being is a physical being and a spiritual being. That spiritual being is the "You", the "I', the "Me"!

Your whole body is a tool to care for and to be used to obey the needs of "You", your soul, the "You"!

Your soul is invisible. In this human world your body is visible. Your invisible soul needs a visible vehicle as a "Tool" as a "Vehicle" and that visible vehicle is your body.

Your physical body has been fashioned in your mother's womb using basic materials from the material world; the mineral, the vegetable and the animal.

Your soul is from the invisible spiritual world of God. Your soul is the energizing and intelligent essence of a human being. Your invisible soul is using the visible body as a material tool in this material world. Your soul which is potentially an intelligent entity is an emanation from the spiritual world.

The body, your body which is a composition of trillions of cells will when the time comes, decompose and its cells will return to the material world it originated from. Therefore the body is mortal. The soul on the other hand is a single entity that does not decompose. Its life is eternal and so the soul is immortal.

The body acts as a tool; as a vehicle for the soul to travel in this human material world. The soul; a potentially intelligent essence, has come to be associated with the human body in order to travel in this world to educate itself; in order to unearth the spiritual qualities potent within it, to build spiritual virtues that can contribute towards the making of the body of mankind on earth a spiritual entity!

To make it clear let us compare the travel of the soul in this material world with that of the growing and developing child in the mother's womb-world. The mother's womb-world is also part of this material world, but the child living in the womb- world is unaware of the outer human world. What is the purpose for which the child is developing body-faculties and growing in the womb-world of its mother?

The purpose for which the child spends about nine months plus in the womb-world of the mother is to prepare its developing body with body faculties; such faculties the child can use to travel after it leaves the womb-world of the mother and arrive to live in this outer material human world!

In like manner the undeveloped spiritual soul with its potential intelligence, power and capacity spends time in this human material world for X number of years, in order to develop itself; the soul with spiritual virtues to use such virtues both in this world and in the next spiritual world.

The developing body in the womb-world of the mother has no power of choice. It is nature using a plan encompassed in the genes and chromosomes found in the ovum of the mother and the sperm of the father that moulds the human body with all its faculties and appendages, before the developed body comes out during birth, to spend an X number of years as a vehicle for the soul in this human dimension. If for some reason the body has not acquired body-faculties during its stay in the womb-world of the mother, it arrives in this outer world; this human world with deprived body-faculties.

The soul emanates from the Creator in the spiritual world to be associated with the developing body in the womb of the mother. The purpose is to use this human world, to encourage to enthuse, to motivate every human being to develop spiritual virtues for the soul. In this instance the development is not automatic and not through nature. Nature has nothing to do with any process of development of the soul. The soul is given the power of choice which matures at a certain age to know that the time has come to seek to know the Truth! It is when the soul independently investigates and knows the Truth and decides to use this knowledge to live through an X number of years in the human dimension; then it begins to develop spiritual virtues before it exits from this world. If the soul has acquired the requisite spiritual virtues that soul is then known as a spiritual-virtues acquired soul. If on the other hand the soul through the use of wrong choices has not recognized its purpose while in this human dimension and so have not chosen to develop spiritual-virtues it will also enter the spiritual world, but as a spiritual-virtues acquired soul!

The prospect of entering the spiritual world, with a spiritual-virtues-deprived soul to live there eternally is indeed a horrible prospect! If a soul has developed spiritual virtues in this human life, such a soul enters the spiritual world, acquired of spiritual virtues. This configurations can be a happy condition throughout eternity!

It is nature that moulds a body of an infant in the womb-world of its mother. In this human world on the other hand, it is the power of choices made at the time of maturity of an individual that dictates choices and decisions made by the soul to acquire spiritual virtues!

If a soul has to make a decision that is right; for example to develop spiritual virtues, in order to arrive at such a decision, a right choice, using right knowledge can influence the making of right decision. Where can the soul receive right knowledge from? In order to influence making right decisions the soul might well ask: *"If the purpose for which I live as a spiritual entity; the soul, and if it is to develop spiritual faculties or virtues before I enter the next spiritual world, from where can I source this knowledge about my invisible soul?"*

This is an intelligent, investigative question. This is a searching question used by seekers who wish to know. "Who am I?"

When the time comes; when the time is right; when the soul is ripe to know, when that soul is destined to know, the answer comes in many ways to every human being on planet earth.

The fact of the matter is that all human beings at sometime in their life from some source, knowledge about the reality of a human being will arrive. But how many will want to investigate on their own about the "Message" they have received?

When the answer comes to a soul seeking to know about the "meaning of life as a human being" the message comes to inform the seeker that the Almighty God has sent a Divine Message to all human beings in this Day! Somehow, somewhere, at some appointed time through somebody or through some agency, the Message arrives for the one who seeks and ready to want to "independently investigate such a Message"!

Chapter 3

What is the source of right knowledge shared in this book?

The reader might well know, that NOW is that time to begin to investigate to want to know right answers from right sources!

So let us begin to investigate the source of right knowledge!

Everything in this world that we can perceive with our senses is either created by man or by God! Man can only create what can be perceived by the human senses. For example a table is created. It is created by a man known as a carpenter. The carpenter has created the table so that it can fulfill a purpose.

The soul of a human being is also created. It is an invisible entity. The One who has Created is also an unknown and an invisible entity known by many Names and here we shall name this invisible One, God. God created the soul. If the soul is a created entity, then for what purpose is a soul created? Only a creator, just like a carpenter who created the table can know why the table has been created! Only God, Who has created the soul of a human being, can know why that soul has been created.

The carpenter can inform the user of the table about the purpose for which the table has been created. How can God who is unknown and invisible reveal the purpose for which the soul is created? Since the true reality of a human being is the soul and if that human being is not informed about the purpose why the soul has been created, will it not be an injustice of the part of the Creator? It is impossible and surely a heresy to even think that God will be unjust!

So how did the Loving Creator; God, Who created us with love made provisions to inform His creation; we human beings to know the purpose of creating the soul?

The answer lies in the fact that He, God once in every thousand or two thousand years uses a special Soul, known to human beings as a Prophet or a Messenger of God to transmit His Message to His creation; human beings!

The Prophet or Messenger of God is used as a Transmitter by God who transmits from an invisible world, His Message also known as the Word of God to human beings. He transmits a Message to all human beings. It is only those who seek to want to know answers to questions like; "Why am I created? Why am I, a soul created? For what purpose am I created as a soul?" who will begin to independently investigate!

As long as the human part of the Prophet or Messenger of God is alive and living amongst His followers, He the Prophet or Messenger of God continues to reveal the Message of God. Once the human part of the Prophet or Messenger of God dies His revealed Message is recorded in a Book, known as the Holy Book of God. As the years pass by those who follow the Teachings of the Holy Book of God become the animating source of a religion. The new-born religion then crystallizes into a civilization. When we investigate further we will come to know that every civilization has its central figure a Prophet or a Messenger of God.

As long as a true seeker independently and prayerfully study the Holy Book of God and live in deeds by the laws and principles revealed therein, assuredly the soul of that individual will develop spiritual virtues and not only live in this human world in heavenly conditions but will also live in heavenly conditions in the spiritual world!

In the physical absence of a Prophet or Messenger of God the true source of right knowledge is the Holy Book of God of that religion. The striving seeker goes all the way to read and understand the Word of God in that Holy Book. The striving seeker becomes aware that the soul's eternal existence begin with knowing The Creator and also knowing the Message He has sent and now found in the Holy Book of that religion!

At this point of time it will be of assistance to the reader to know that all sources of right knowledge shared in this book is from the many Holy Books of God known to man in this age! No knowledge is shared in this book that is gleaned from interpretations of the Holy Books of God!

Chapter 4

How can I know that I am a spiritual being?

A human being is composed of two entities. One is a physical being; the body. The second is a spiritual being; the soul.

The physical being is a visible body, and the spiritual being is an invisible soul.

The controller of actions of a human being is not the body. The controller of actions of a human being is the soul.

The physical aspect of a human being; the body is only a tool. The body which is a tool used by the soul is for the purpose of the soul to experience living in this world amongst human beings to educated itself during this lifetime, by developing the soul's God-given potential qualities; spiritual virtues while living as a human being!

Whatever happens to the body in health and sickness in comfort and in pain is experienced by the soul.

God has enabled a human being In order to be educated about the existence of the soul is the event known as a dream. In a dream the sleeping human being "sees" and "experiences" travelling to strange and not so strange places whilst the body is still lying on a bed. What is travelling? What is that entity that is travelling without the use of the body? It is the soul of a human being. It is your soul! That is the "You".

Your body has five outer senses. Your soul also has five inner senses. Your soul experiences, educates itself, learns and develops spiritual virtues by using the body's five outer senses.

Your soul arrived to be associated with the developing body in the womb-world of the mother at the time when the ovum of the mother and the sperm of the father met and became fertilized to become a zygote.

Your soul when it came to be associated with the developing body in the womb-world of the mother; it arrived to begin its travel as a pure and undeveloped "seed". This soul in the form of a "seed" animated by the human spirit is responsible to energize the development and growth of the human body in the womb-world of the mother; a body which will ultimately become a tool or a vehicle to be used by the soul to travel in the next human world.

The soul experiences whatever happens in the material world by using the five senses of the body to which it is associated. For example the eyes of the body do not see. It is the soul using the eyes of the body as a tool that sees.

The soul is not "in the body". The soul is associated with the body. As an example of this association; the remote control of a television monitor is not in the television set. But there is a connection between the monitor and the television set. This connection of the remote control with the television set is what is meant by association. The soul is associated with the body in this manner.

It is through this association with the body, using the bodily senses, that the soul feels and experiences spiritual qualities that enables the soul to develop spiritual virtues or faculties. To develop spiritual virtues, rather than non-spiritual virtues the soul is given the "power of choice". Using this power to choose, the soul which decides to develop spiritual virtues shuns anything that leads to negate the development of spiritual virtues.

To explain more in detail the mechanism of association of the soul and the body let us study an example.

We know that there is a "connection" between the remote control of a television set and the television monitor. We also know that we cannot see this invisible connection but know that it is there. Science teaches us that the connection is a bundle of electrical vibrations. We know that it is true because using scientific instruments this invisible, vibrating connection can be monitored and quantified using scientific methods.

It is important to note before we go further to know that science and scientific discoveries deal with things material; that which can be perceived by our five bodily senses. Our body is a material entity. Our soul is a spiritual entity. Our soul being a spiritual entity cannot be proven to exist by scientific means.

When we compare the remote control of the television set to our soul, we must also know that while the remote control is an inorganic thing, the soul on the other had is an independent, thinking and a living entity. The soul besides choosing to evaluate choices that cause to develop its spiritual virtues, it is also an intelligently coordinated bundle of energizing factors that cause to control body functions.

What body functions your soul wishes or choose to energize and coordinate will depend entirely upon the choices the soul makes. If it is the choice of the soul to use the body to attach itself and bring about material benefits it can do so and the soul then becomes a material entity and the human being a materially orientated person.

If the soul on the other hand chooses to energize the body tool to execute affairs in life using spiritual means in order to develop the soul with spiritual virtues one becomes a spiritually orientated person.

While living as a human being with a purpose to fulfill the right choices to make in our daily affairs, it must be in line with, to "*Walk the mystical path, with practical feet*".

Chapter 5

Where have I come from?

This is a question every human being must ask oneself at some point of time in their life. The answers to this question have come from varied sources and upon investigation it has been found that the answers were only interpretations of individuals who transmitted their own understanding and who think that they know all the answers!

The true answer to this question is found only in all the Holy Books of God. All other answers are but conjectures. Such an anomaly has come about because the formal educational format used worldwide has not included a "missing link" in its chain!

There are many reasons why this "missing link" was excluded and this is not the place or time to enumerate the causes.

This book is written in order to share with every human being on earth, right knowledge of the Highway of Life one will have to travel, in order to reach the desired destination.

All answers and answers to questions seekers ask, that have not been extracted truthfully from the "missing link" have resulted in many souls travelling along a highway of life that can only lead them to arrive at a destination that can result in them experiencing and living in eternal remorse. This is the Truth!

You are now aware that you are a "SOUL". The real YOU is the soul. Your soul is associated with your body-vehicle. It is your soul that is travelling in this human dimension on planet earth.

As a human being you are a BODY and a SOUL. The body has been developed with body-faculties while it was in the womb-world of the mother. Therefore the body has come from the womb-world of the mother.

The Soul on the other hand is a spiritual entity. The soul has come from the spiritual world. The soul has emanated from the Creator; God. This emanation can be compared to a painting that has emanated from the artist or a woodwork that has emanated from the carpenter.

The soul that has emanated from God has within it, in a potential form, all the attributes and qualities of God. Love, forgiveness, mercy, honesty, truthfulness, which are all spiritual in nature, are attributes and qualities of God. The soul which becomes associated with the zygote in the womb of the mother is undeveloped, pure and undefiled. It comes as a "seed". Just as a seed has within it, in a potential form, all the qualities of the tree, the soul which can be compared to a seed has within it, all the attributes and qualities of God.

Everything that is created by God has its destined place in the map of creation. Everything that has been created by God has a pre-destined purpose to fulfill. Everything that has been created by God lives and moves according to a specific law suited for its existence.

In creation ONLY a human being has been given the power of choice to do whatever he or she chooses to do! A human being is free to make any choice and then decide to transform such a choice into deeds. But if a choice is made that deviates from the law of God, the result will assuredly attract dire consequences.

The dire consequences in the form of suffering, pain, tragedy, and living in fear by the generality of mankind in this day, is as a result of human beings making and living wrong choices.

Since it is now common knowledge that a human being is truly a spiritual reality; the real you, I, or me being the soul, it can now be possible to answer the question, "Where have I come from?" The soul has come from God; from the unknown and invisible spiritual world. The invisible soul in order to travel in this visible material world has to have a vehicle that is visible and that vehicle is the human body.

Having known the truth about the body and the soul and its relationship with one another as the soul travels in this human dimension the time has come to study further to know for what reasons has the soul come to be associated with the body to travel in this human dimension on planet earth.

We end this chapter with a right answer to the question; "Where have I come from?"

"I the invisible soul, have come from God as an emanation of the Creator, as a spiritual seed, pure, undefiled and undeveloped, in order to travel in the human dimension and using the body and its faculties as a visible vehicle to travel in this human dimension, to be spiritually educated, to choose to make attempts to develop my potentially created spiritual virtues, to enable me to reach at the end of my journey in this world to continue to live in the spiritual world eternally nearer to God in heavenly conditions".

Chapter 6

Why do I need spiritual faculties?

'Why do I need spiritual faculties?" This is an interesting and a searching question. Many out there will not want to ask this question. To many the task of developing material lifestyles is already a daunting task. If they are asked to also concentrate on developing spiritual qualities or spiritual virtues, they will not be interested. Perhaps, if they know the importance of developing spiritual virtues during the X number of years they still have, before they leave this world; perhaps they will become interested. There are also some who after knowing why they should also prioritize developing spiritual virtues, and still do not wish to pursue this task, they must know that it was a choice they made. Assuredly such souls who wish to remain ignorant of the importance to develop spiritual virtues when they can, will at the end of their journey in this life, surely will face eternity with eternal remorse. As you continue to read this book you will know why a warning of this nature couched with love has been made!

To be able to answer this question about the soul which is an invisible, unknown entity, let us try to relate this question using a known parallel. The unknown entity is the soul. The known entity is the body of the child from the womb-world of the mother. Such an enquiry will lead us to know to understand better the answer to the question, *"Why do I need spiritual qualities?"*

We know about the human body. The human body originated and developed body-qualities in the womb-world of the mother. The womb-world of the mother is not a permanent place for the body of the developing child. The purpose why the body had to be in the womb-world of the mother for nine months plus, is to enable the body to develop body faculties, like eyes, ears, nose, limbs, organs etc. so that when the body leaves the womb-world of the mother and enters the human world, these body faculties will be of assistance for the body to live a functional life and become a perfect vehicle for the soul to travel in this human world.

We now know why the body in the womb-world of the mother has to develop body-faculties before it arrives to enter this human world. It is also important to note that body-faculties develop in the womb-world of the mother and after birth those body faculties that were developed in the womb-world of the mother will grow as the child grows to become a youth, then an adult and into old age. Body faculties that did not develop in the womb-world of the mother cannot develop after leaving the womb-world and entering the world outside it; the human world. For example if eyes for the child while it was still in the womb-world of the mother did not develop, that child will enter this world as a blind child and will remain as long as it lives as a blind person deprived of eye-sight!

Since we now know from the known about the necessity of the child in the womb-world of the mother to develop body-faculties before it arrives in this outer human world, it will now be easy to understand why the soul needs to develop spiritual qualities while travelling in this human world from birth to death!.

Development by the soul of spiritual qualities or virtues will have to be undertaken by the soul while it still remains associated with the body in this human dimension. While in this human dimension the soul can develop spiritual qualities. Once the soul leaves the human dimension to enter the spiritual world beyond, the soul cannot develop any spiritual qualities. To repeat: Development of spiritual virtues by the soul; by YOU, can only be achieved while travelling in this human dimension.

It is absolutely important that you understand this true fact.

Imagine your body arriving in this human dimension deprived of eyesight. You are then known as a blind person. Will you wish or wish for anyone else to suffer such a deprivation? Of course you will never want such an eventuality to happen!

If a child is born blind, it will continue to live in this human dimension, but will spend its life and progress as a blind person. Every other body-faculty that has been developed in the womb-world of the mother will grow in this outer human dimension and become useful to that child but since the eyes did not develop in the womb-world of the mother, it will remain a blind person all its life in this world.

The body faculties the child has developed while the child was still in the womb-world of the mother will grow but will not develop further in this outer human world.

To enable an in-depth understanding of the meaning of development and growth of body or soul faculties, another example will suffice. While the child was developing body faculties in the womb-world of the mother let us suppose that both the arms were not developed. The child will not know what arms are and even if deprived of growth of arms the child could not be aware of this deprivation. After the child enters the outer human dimension the child enters deprived of arms and becomes arms-less. In this outer world it will be impossible for the child to have its arms developed. Though it lives a certain number of years in this human world, all through its life the child lives deprived of arms.

The same conditions apply to the soul. If the soul did not develop spiritual virtues while still living associated with the human body in this human dimension, the soul will leave this world and enter the spiritual world beyond deprived of spiritual virtues. Whereas the child that arrives deprived of body-faculties will suffer this deprivation only for a certain number of years until the death of the body, the soul on the other hand will live deprived of spiritual virtues in the spiritual world through eternity! What a tragedy!

Can we imagine anything worse than to live through eternity deprived of spiritual faculties?

Based on this very same subject let us explore further the consequences of developmental deprivation of either the body or the soul.

Can a child born blind; deprived of eye-sight, and knowing about this deprivation cry out to the mother begging to want to go back into her womb-world to develop eyes? Absurd as it is it can never happen!

In like manner if the soul during its tenure in this material human world did not develop spiritual virtues and upon entering the spiritual world becomes aware of this deprivation and wants to return to this world to make up for the deprivation; can this be possible? Never!

For the child in the womb-world of the mother there is only one precious opportunity to develop body-faculties. In like manner the soul too has only one precious opportunity to develop spiritual virtues while it is associated with the human body in this material world!

This is the reason why the soul of a human being must become aware of this knowledge and strive before it is too late to develop spiritual virtues!

Yet another truth that must be emphasized here is that the development of body faculties of the body of the child in the womb-world of the mother was not choice-related. This child did not know what to develop. This child did not have the luxury of the power of choice. All development was as a result of natures plan! This plan was embedded in the genes and chromosomes of the ova and the sperm.

On the other hand the soul was created and came to associate with the body of the child while it was still in the womb-world of the mother and after birth when the mental faculties ripened upon maturity the power of choice came into play and the soul had full control to choose to develop the soul-virtues.

An important reason why the soul should develop spiritual virtues is to begin to plan to fulfill the purpose for which it was created. Using the developing spiritual virtues the soul begins to reflect its lifestyles in deeds. If the soul has chosen to do the right through deeds; these deeds will reflect right ethics, right morals and right virtues. Such a right lifestyle will cause to transform this world of humankind to become a body that can reflect unity in diversity, peace, prosperity and happiness.

At this juncture you might want to know whether you as an individual can accomplish such a global transformation! You can! As you read on you will understand and know without any doubt that you have been created in this Age to be part of such a global revolution that will bring about a New World Order!

Think deeply about this truth; A drop from the ocean has all the qualities of that ocean within it. In like manner your soul which is an emanation from God has within it, in a potential form, all the qualities of the Creator! All these qualities of God are potentially within the soul as the tree, branches, flowers and fruits are potentially created and waiting to emerge from the seed of that tree!

As the soul makes right choices to want to develop spiritual virtues which are created and await its emergence into the human world through deeds; it is then the world will see the light of unity, peace, prosperity and happiness of all that dwell on earth!

At this juncture in our narrative about the unknown and invisible soul and the methodology used to make the unknown known it is important to know that the material world we live in is truly an illusion while the spiritual world is the world of reality! The spiritual world is the world of "light" whist the material world is a world of "shadow". Every entity in the material world has a counterpart in the spiritual world. Attachment to the material world; attachment to things material is like attaching to an illusion; attaching to a shadow that has no substance!

Objective things we sense in the material world can be described using material language. On the other hand subjective entities or spiritual realities cannot be described to be understood using material language. Sciences belong to the material world. Therefore in order to make known spiritual realities, a counterpart in the material world is used.

An example to make known what is meant in the afore-mentioned paragraph will be useful. Take for example a "seed". As long as the seed has not germinated or come to life, it is looked upon as a seed that is "dead". In the Holy Books the soul is likened to a seed. If the soul has come to life it is then known as a living soul. On the other hand if the soul has not come to life, it is known as a dead soul.

The greatest tragedy that has resulted in relation to the True Religion of God is when the Revealed Word of God in the Holy Books of God is hijacked and then translated or interpreted literally according to the translators understanding or the interpreters understanding!

Spiritual truth can only be described using analogies and parables. When these symbolic descriptions of the Revealed Word of God are interpreted literally; it is then the beginning of confusion and the appearance of sects which result in disunity and become the cause of anger, hate, fights, wars and consequent pain and suffering!

If you wish to know about the invisible and unknown soul read the authentic Holy Books! Then compare the creation and qualities of the spiritual soul, with the material seed and study step by step how the seed fulfills its purpose. This approach can assist you to know much more about our soul and the purpose of its creation!

Chapter 7

You came into this world as a seed

In this chapter, for an in-depth comprehension of the subject *"dealing with knowing the unknown, through studying the known"* let us deal with situations using some more comparisons.

We are now aware that a human being is an association of both; a physical material being and a spiritual being: the soul.

Using our material knowledge we can understand what a body; a physical being is. If we wish to understand what a soul is like and for what purpose it is created we should use the seed as an example. This is because knowledge about how the seed fulfils its purpose will give us some understanding about the methodologies to be involved to assure how the soul has to fulfill the purpose of its creation!

Let us not forget that the seed fulfills its purpose according to laws established by the Creator; natural laws that make the seed to fulfill its purpose when certain conditions are met.

To remind ourselves once again, we will have keep in mind that In order to understand spiritual truth we will have to know the fact that since material knowledge cannot describe in material language, spiritual truths the only means to try to understand is to study what parallel there is in the material world we know about.. So, this is a sure means to want to know about our spiritual soul.

The easiest means that can open a window to know about spirituality is to use parables and anecdotes that are used to describe a subjective unknown entity.

A spiritual truth and the mechanisms involved in spiritual matters, when compared to a like situation existing in nature can give us an understanding as to what it could be!. All too often this manner of trying to understand the unknown creates insights into the mode of operation of matters spiritual.

Someone tells you, "*My heart is broken*". If you use a literal meaning to understand what is said, you know for sure that one whose heart is broken will not live to tell you about it. The person is using a story trying to inform you that a love relationship has come to an end. Since *love* is a spiritual entity which cannot be described objectively the only way to express the deep sorrow one feels because of falling out of love is to use a means of expression like, *"My heart is broken"* to indicate the hopelessness of the feeling experienced.

As we study the spiritual world, we will find that The Creator had placed meaningful twin similarities, one in the spiritual world and another in the natural or material world. This is done, to enable truth-seekers to make attempts to sincerely search and understand the mystic signs.

The soul...the undeveloped soul is compared to a seed. The seed is also undeveloped. For the seed to fulfill the purpose of its creation there are certain conditions to be fulfilled, before the apparently "dead" seed comes to "life"...; and germinates and develops the potential powers within it!

When the soul arrives, to be associated with the developing body in the womb, it is apparently "dead" . The apparently "dead" soul has to come to life, before it develops, the potentials created within it.

A seed has to be sown in fertile conditions and then it should be exposed to the life-giving power of the physical sun. Then it starts to germinate and progress to be a fruiting tree.

The soul too, has to find itself associated with a human being qualified with a non-prejudiced, God-fearing, soil of the heart. When it has found this quality it has to then expose itself to the life-giving power of the Light of the Spiritual Sun, (The Word of God) before it comes to life. This process is often referred to as being "born again"!

Once these two important criteria for the seed to germinate is fulfilled, the seed then begins to "be born again" and this means that the latent powers within it will see that it grows into a tree with branches, leaves, flowers and fruits. The seed then achieves "second birth". The seed has fulfilled the purpose for which it has been created!

The undeveloped soul comes to associate with the developing body in the womb-world of the mother. When the two criteria (That is, once it becomes associated with a non-prejudiced, God-fearing, soil of the heart of a human being and then exposes itself to the life-giving Word of

God), is fulfilled, the soul will then begin to stir to "come to life".

In obedience to the command of God, (The Word of God which is likened to the Rays of the Spiritual Sun), the soul will then begin to develop all necessary spiritual faculties. After that the soul will become the Spirit of Faith, just as a seed becomes a seedling. When this happens the soul which is now known as the spirit of Faith, will then choose to study the Word of God and begins to reflect in thoughts, words and deeds the fruits of The New Age. These fruits are the moral and ethical values. In time to come the living of such a lifestyle can bring about a New World Order, in which men and women all over the world, will live in unity amongst diversity, and this will contribute towards the establishment of Global Peace, Prosperity and Happiness of all mankind!

It is now absolutely clear, that unless and until the soul (that is you), have *developed spiritual faculties, you will not and cannot, fulfill the purpose for* which you have been created and sent, to spend a lifetime in the human dimension.

It has been said, that, "A tree without fruit, is fit for the fire." As such, a soul without development of spiritual faculties is headed for damnation!

In the case of the seed, it is the life-giving, growth-initiating power of nature that instigates and dictates its development to become a fruit-bearing tree. Where the soul is concerned, it is the power of the choice of the soul itself, to decide, as to whether it wishes to act to develop spiritual faculties or not. This we must know! Amongst all of creation it is only the soul, that is YOU....who has been created with the power to choose! Do not forget that! You are not nature. Nature has no choice! You have the choice to do what you want to do; even to disobey God! Isn't that frightening?

You, the soul's travel time, in this human dimension is restricted to a certain number of years. After that, you step out of this human dimension and enter into the next spiritual dimension. In the spiritual dimension, your soul will live an eternal life.

This is the reason why the life of a soul in this human dimension is so important. This is the reason why you have to develop as much spiritual faculties in this life in this human dimension, during the limited time you have.

The condition (heavenly condition or hellish condition) of your eternal existence in the spiritual world will depend upon the quantum of development of your soul.

Can you afford not to heed this warning? Can you afford to strive all the days of your life to be a material giant in this world and continue to live as a spiritual non-entity? Can you afford to take this risk, not knowing when your journey in this world will end?

Now it is clear to you that you will not die. You know that you are the soul; not the body! You are the soul and the soul is immortal. The soul is a living entity and what must concern you..... Is the condition of YOU, the soul, once it leaves this earthly, human dimension in this material world and enters the next spiritual world!.

Therefore, there is no reason why you should be afraid of the body dying. It has to happen and it will happen. In the end this body of yours which came from the mineral world will decompose and return from where it came; the mineral world! There is nothing you or anyone can do to stop this from happening! As such fear of death is futile!

If you are afraid of your body dying before you have enough time to develop spiritual faculties... then that is what you should be afraid of! You should be afraid of the fact that you will, because of the wrong choices you made in this life; because you have not developed your spiritual faculties while living in this world you will assuredly leave this world as a "dead soul". If this happens according to universal law you will be attracted to enter the spiritual world, as a "dead" soul!

You should be afraid if you have committed any crime, knowing that the crime you committed would have caused certain damage to your soul. You should be afraid if you have not learned lessons from transgressions you have committed! You should be afraid when you come to realize that once you enter the spiritual world, you will have no choice to right the wrong! You should be afraid wondering when will the last moment of your existence in this life come about; when you will have to end your journey in this life, and whether by that time, you would have developed your soul! You should be afraid when you realize that this life is only the second stage of your travel and it is only in this stage that you can do what you are expected to do; to prepare YOU; the soul for your eternal life and living in all the various infinite worlds of God! You should be afraid to note the fact that if you had not chosen to develop spiritual faculties of your soul in this life, you will have to live through eternity, with only what you have developed in this life; nothing more, nothing less! Frightening, but it is the TRUTH!

Once again in order to impress your mind, using Truth, about the purpose of your life while you are living in this human dimension, never forget that you are here to be spiritually educated first, and all the rest of the education comes second to it!

Animals need not be educated to survive in this world. Animals are instinctively programmed. You, on the other hand, have to be educated to know how to fulfill the purpose of your being created. At the same time you need to be educated to know how to care for your body-vehicle and this is where material education fits in!

Most people, including you, who live in this world in this human dimension, do not know this fact, this Truth! It is not too late! If you can be sure that you have some more days, weeks, months, years to live, you have a choice! How can you be sure? Even now you can make a decision to know, what you should do, and what you should not do, in order to develop spiritual faculties. Do it now!

You have to live a lifestyle guided by right spiritual knowledge in order to develop your soul with spiritual faculties. You have to do that NOW! Don't you want to enter Paradise in the next Spiritual World? Don't you? Then you have to do something about it. This is not a "wishing" exercise. Yours is a "must do" exercise! There is no other way!

Imagine being born blind….. This is not as bad as you think. As a blind person you have not developed your eyes in the womb of your mother. As mentioned earlier, you are well aware that you cannot develop your eyes upon entering the human dimension and as an adult or even as a Ruler, you will still be visually impaired.... For how long? For a certain number of years perhaps? *Yes, only a certain number of years.*

The difference between entering the human dimension blind and entering the spiritual world "blind" is this; that if you are blind in the human dimension you have the power of choice to do something or anything of your choice to live immersed in blindness. But if you are "born" into the spiritual world you will have no choice at all to better your condition. The power of choice ends at the point of death of the body!

Now read the following very carefully!

When you leave this human life and enter the next life in the spiritual world, without developing the spiritual faculties of your soul, you will then spend an eternal life in the infinite spiritual worlds of God... but how? As a deprived soul! You will progress, but you will progress as a soul deprived of spiritual faculties!

A blind, deaf, dumb, and deformed body is a body deprived of proper body faculties' development. This development should have been completed during the nine months plus, while the body was in the womb-world of the mother.

If the soul whilst traveling in this human dimension has not made a choice to develop spiritual faculties, assuredly it will leave this world deprived and it will continue to progress through eternity in the very same deprived condition.

Now it is left to you, to choose to either develop your soul, or not to develop your soul. Know that; you and you alone, are responsible for the development of your soul!

Chapter 8

Your Spiritual Education

You are now aware that you must be exposed to spiritual education.

You need spiritual education because you are actually a spiritual being. It is only through spiritual education can you know who you truly are. It is only through education will you know why you are created as a human being. It is only through spiritual education will you know for what purpose you were created. It is only though spiritual education will you be able to know how you can fulfill the purpose for which you were created. It is only though spiritual education you will know why you have been created to live as a human being on planet earth in this Day of all Days!

There can be no two ways about this!

What are the two ways? One is to know the Truth as revealed in all Scriptural Writings (and now simplified in this book) and two, to disregard what you are reading now, and to go on living the way you have always done! The choice is entirely yours!

To those who wish to know more about spiritual education and who truly desire to know and understand the Truth, and wish to immediately change course and take the right Highway of Life, please read on! If not you can choose to set aside reading this book!

A booklet entitled, "9 Steps to Paradise", from this writer will give you, a dynamic perspective about living a balanced lifestyle and at the same time share with you the knowledge as to how to develop your soul with spiritual faculties! You are advised to read this booklet, for basic in-depth information about this most important subject about the ways to begin to develop your soul and this by choosing to live according to Truth!

The spiritual education of any human being has to begin the moment you become associated with the developing zygote in the womb of your mother. Your mother, who is supported in this exercise by your father and your family members, initiates this education. The mode of this education is through the link created between your mind; the mind of YOU as the soul when it is still in the condition of a "seed" and the mind of your mother!

This mode of spiritual education, with the mother as the first spiritual educator is the beginning of all true education! While you; (as the soul), become associated with the developing body in your mother's womb, through this mind-connection, you will be able to experience feelings of whatever pictures your mother impresses in her mind. You will be able to experience your mother's feelings as she experiences different life-situations. This is the beginning of your spiritual education. That is why your mother is your first teacher; spiritual teacher!

What the mother sees with her eyes is imprinted in her mind as a picture. This picture is relayed to the mind of the developing child in her womb. The child will not understand what the picture is all about. What the child will associate with the picture is the feeling the mother experiences when she imprints the feelings-related picture which she unknowingly and naturally transmits to the mind of her child developing in her womb.

Whether the mother experiences joy or fear, these experiences are registered in the mind and memory of the developing child in the womb. Even various sounds are imprinted in the mind of the developing child. When the child is born into this world the soul can be able to recognize such sounds and associate it with either joy or fear!

That is why it is very important that the mother during pregnancy, lead a lifestyle conducive to imprinting right impressions on to the mental make-up of the developing child within her womb.

It is also important, that the father be loving, sharing and caring, as a support to the mother in this spiritual exercise.

To cite as an example; a truthful statement thought over and vocalized by the mother is a right and a positive statement. This is a right and a positive spiritual input which is stored in the mind of the developing child. A lie vocalized by the mother is a negative, useless but also a powerful statement which will also be retained in the mind of the developing child within! If that lie evokes feelings the input will be even greater. Reflecting truth in ones life which generates feelings of joy and happiness, of strength and courage are what should influence the mind of the growing child. On the other hand living a lifestyle peppered as a matter of fact of wrong and negative habit-patterns will cause feelings of fear and wretchedness, weakness and cowardice.

The mother will have to shoulder the responsibility to mould the mind of the yet unborn child. Whether she wishes to bring forth an upright noble human being or a sleazy downtrodden outcast, will be her choice and hers alone!

A casual study of the type of lifestyle that is prevailing in the world today, will make it clear to any observer that a vast majority of human beings in this day are living lives worse than that of animals in the wild!

Another informal study of the pattern of lifestyles that is lived by the majority of peoples on planet earth, amongst many other examples, is the glaring discrimination practiced by men over women anywhere!

If this discriminatory attitude is practiced towards women, Is it then difficult to recognize and isolate the cause of all the ills that is now crippling the body of humankind? Is it then difficult to recognize how deprivation of proper education of women who will one day be mothers of their children has resulted in children born without the benefit of early spiritual education?

From the moment all the peoples on planet earth follow the Truth and agree that in the eyes of the Maker, man and woman are equal. That the only difference is in the anatomical structure and physiological methodology between the two. That this difference is to enable the facilitation by the women to propagate the human race. If everyone recognizes this Truth, then this world will begin to see the dawning of everyone living noble lifestyles, in unity, peace, prosperity and happiness!

Is it not unity, peace and prosperity that this world for centuries is hungering for and has been looking forward to happen? Is this not the Truth? Will we not, as a passing generation in this day be proud to give to our children and future generations, as a befitting gift to them, a world, that is seeing the dawn of unity, peace, prosperity and happiness? Is this not what decent human beings will long for; to leave behind a precious gift after they end their striving and travelling in this human dimension? Is this not what will make the soul happy; happy to realize that in the end, in obedience to the laws and principles revealed by the Creator, your soul's entry into the spiritual world beyond, will earn a rightful place as a fully developed soul?

Now that it is truthfully explained that discrimination in any way in the name of gender prejudice will cause great harm to the soul of any human being who practice it, may a new mind-set become the cause to generate right thoughts, words and deeds amongst humankind!

It is possible to begin now to educate women in this age to convey to their minds that they can indeed play a vital, uplifting and an energizing role in the affairs of mankind. Can this fact be doubted anymore? If one is looking for the cause of the degradation of human kind in this Day, let them not look too far! It is happening right in front of them, in their own backyards, in nearly every place on planet earth! The cause? Gender prejudice! This is it! May leaders take note!

This is the reason why a mother should be a spiritually educated person! This is such an important factor in the making of a progressive, united, prosperous and a happy civilization. Educating a girl is so important, so much so that, if a parent has two children, a boy and a girl and can educate only one... the girl must be educated first!

If a woman intends to marry and has no spiritual education, it is far better not to be married, and not bring forth children!

Words cannot suffice to adequately express the great station of a woman especially a mother! A true mother will submit and happily be a part to all forms of sacrifice in order to nurture a child, right from her womb until maturity! Study the history of mankind, and you will find that great and prosperous civilizations existed when a woman was in the driving seat!

In the eyes of the Creator, it is not the gender that He supports, but a pure and a noble heart. Any heart whether it is that of a man or a woman who lives in obedience to His laws and Principles attracts His love!

Therefore, viewing the right station of women and the treatment of women in this age is of great importance! Women deserve to be treated with high regard, with respect, with love, and with genuine concern for their well being.

In fact, one of the ways to damage one's soul is to deny women the right of equal opportunity in every aspect of human affairs. To marry a woman and abandon her is a great sin that will cause the soul to be deformed and deprived! This does not mean that only men can be faulted. Women, in general, who experience a certain liberating force, and this, causing the breaking of the chains that had shackled them for countless years and now free to play their rightful role in human society, must be more careful not to avenge the perpetrators who have once degraded them! However, they must be doubly wary about their independence, lest they use this emancipation, as a tool to unleash their bottled anger, to hurt men!

Women are much more resilient and patient under stress, and therefore they must, because of their superior inner strength, support and guide men to view and overcome challenges with greater compassion and patience!

Imagine then, with what tender loving care can an educated mother, well versed in spiritual education, bring forth a child that will ultimately become an asset in the body of mankind! Until men in particular, understand the value of women and the role they can play, in uniting humanity (a pre-requisite to bring about Universal Peace), can the prosperity and happiness of the body of mankind, be achieved!

The body of mankind is suffering from all forms of illnesses, caused by disobedience to the Laws and Principles of God's Teachings. Men in this Day, must immediately take steps to support and encourage, the participation of women as consultative partners in all their deliberations in order to rectify and prevent the ugly situations that prevail in this Day!

It is no exaggeration to state, that there is very little time left, before, both men and women as a whole, understand the role of women and so cause to change mind-sets, before further damage is done to the body of mankind. If this advice is not heeded the result will be unthinkable; appalling, destructive and will bring about deadly chaos around the planet! Will this generation be proud when a blighted future is handed over to our children and future generations?

No one in the right mind should judge human potential based on gender. Only the ignorant and prejudiced will stoop so low! It will be these kinds of people who adopt gender prejudice, who will join the ranks of those who leave this world with a deprived soul!

Nowhere in the volumes of Writings revealed by Prophets and Messengers of God, has there been a quote on gender-bias! Why then, should anyone in this enlightened age, treat women as second-class citizens? It is time to stop this gender-prejudice! We have to advocate to stop this discrimination NOW!

Chapter 9

How You Unwittingly Damage Your Soul

Ill-treating women, depriving women of their God-given rights, abandoning women after marrying them, indulging in rape and incest, practicing brute force to subdue women, using status and gender prejudice to seduce and spoiling women, deceiving to entice adulterous practice where the woman is the aggrieved party...... all these habit-patterns project the animal nature in man which can damage the soul.

In these days you will find that many women also take over these roles to subjugate men. Either way there is no doubt whatsoever about the considerable damage done to the soul of the person involved. This damage can prevent the normal spiritual development of the soul, resulting in the soul at the time it leaves this life, becoming attracted to live under hellish conditions throughout eternity.

Parents should not shelter under the belief that their children belong to them! In truth our children do not belong to us. Our children are God-sent. Children are given to parents as a gift of trust from God. If you are a parent, and wish to protect the trust of God placed under your care, then bring up your children and nurture them even from their infancy to practice obedience to parents and teachers. Teach them the knowledge of God. If you have neglected these tasks, you will have damaged your soul!

To live a life deprived of ethics and morals, whether in the home, in the school, in colleges, universities, workplace etc. will naturally contribute towards extensive damage to the soul! For the sake of a goodly eternal life, we should think and refrain from living such ungodly lives!

Backbiting and gossip can cause serious damage to the soul, of both the gossiper and also the listener, who encourages the gossiper by listening!

Cheating, dishonesty, lying, alcoholism and being a victim of drug abuse are other potent causes that will surely damage the soul! In fact drugs can "kill" the soul!

It is not practical to relate within the ambit of this handy book to enumerate many more reasons that can contribute towards damaging the soul. In fact every transgression; which is disobeying and doing things contrary to the guidance of God are causes that will damage the soul.

Suffice it to state categorically here and now, that unless and until at the end of your journey in this life, your soul is developed or not developed, acquired of spiritual virtues or deprived of spiritual virtues, you will assuredly be attracted according to the quantum of development of spiritual virtues to that level of eternal existence where you spend your ongoing eternal life either in heavenly conditions or in hellish conditions!

Whether you are living eternally in heavenly conditions or eternally in hellish conditions, you, the soul, will still progress in the spiritual world, but your progress will only be in state, but not in condition. To make a comparison; if you are born blind, which means you are deprived of sight, you can still progress in state, as a blind individual and even become somebody in this world, but you will still remain in a condition of blindness!

Now you are aware of what can and will happen, to your soul, and how you have the power and enduring capacity to make right choices and decide to in deeds reflect in action the nature of the choices you make. Living such a lifestyle can enable you to want and to live an eternal life in heavenly conditions. Otherwise you will end up to live eternally in hellish conditions. Whatever happens to you in the afterlife is wholly and entirely dependent upon the choices you make while you are still living and travelling in the human world on planet earth.

Now you know how the choices to live the life you decide upon in this human world can either give you eternal joy when you leave this world or eternal remorse when you realize at the hour of death the mistakes you made by choosing to refrain from independently investigate Truth in order to live right lifestyles!

Now that you know the Truth, do you still want to disobey the Laws and Principles enshrined in the Teachings of God; Teachings that are enshrined in the Holy Books of God?

After understanding the nature of consequences you will attract if you do not live lives in obedience to God's Teachings, you will surely want to independently investigate to know what is right and what is wrong, what to choose and what not to choose; choices that can guarantee development of your soul or make choices to remain heedless even when the consequence of such irresponsibility is to leave this human dimension with a deprived soul to live an eternity in eternal remorse!

Where can you find the Teachings of God? You can find them in all the true Holy Scriptures, sent by God periodically in intervals of a thousand or two thousand years through His Prophets and Messengers.

When do you begin to investigate? Now! There is no tomorrow for any one of us! Remember, September 11, 2001? Was there a tomorrow for the thousands who perished on that day? Did they know that the end of their journey in this world has arrived? There is a lesson in this event we have to learn!

Chapter 10

Remember Sept.11, 2001?

On that fateful day, September 11, 2001, the whole of humanity was shocked, to watch live, the killing of thousands of workers, guests and visitors within minutes, in the famous Twin Towers in New York, The message this tragic incident proclaimed to all humanity is that there is a today but not tomorrow for you or for anyone one else living in this day on planet earth! How many would have seen or heard of this event to realize that in this happening there is a potent and a timely message to all humanity?

You did not ask to be born as a human being. You will also not, know, when your journey in this dimension will end! The fact and the Truth is that when death comes, it comes unheralded! Will you be ready at that time? Will your soul be developed with spiritual virtues at that time?

When you end your journey in this human dimension, will you be ready to enter the next spiritual dimension, with a developed soul? Will you; your soul, be ready and developed, to be attracted to levels where you can eternally live in heavenly conditions?

This is the voice of Truth! Only you can truly give the right answer. You and only you are responsible, for the development of your soul!

How sad it is when we recollect and realize, that throughout your life as a human being, you had spend your time, money, energy, skills and talents to develop your body's attachment to the things of this world; things which satisfy your senses, without realizing that all the things of this world you have exerted and sacrificed for to achieve, will one day end when your body is buried or at the burning fire if you body is cremated! What can you then take with you, to the next world? Can your wealth, your property, your status, the attachments you have lived for, be taken along with you? No! Then why not understand that, from the moment you entered this life, into this materially rich world, you were slowly leaving it behind. Then use whatever time you still have to focus, choose and decide to act as to how to develop your immortal soul!?

September 11, 2001, has taught the world a lesson. The lesson is to be prepared at all times, because no one can predict when the end will come! How many amongst the thousands, would have made plans for the morrow; how many would have promised their spouses, their children, their near and dear ones about their plans for the future; why even that evening? Within minutes their tomorrows had vanished!

If you had not thought about this horrendous happening, in this manner, or interpreted it as a warning to the still living, then the time has come for you to look at it, as a message specially sent to you, from a Loving Creator! Is there any other way to understand why this tragedy had happened?

What then is the prescription that can cure the diseases that cause an undeveloped soul to enter the next dimension?

The prescription is spiritual education!

Now is the time to begin to educate the world, about the Creator. Now is the time to learn how the One Creator created all things in the cosmos, and together with such vast creation, He also created human beings with so much love. This He did, so that mankind may know Him! He also created mankind to know Him and to know His Teachings both spiritual and social, to enable His children, to do His Will and to go back to Him after developing their souls with spiritual virtues. These spiritual virtues enrich the soul to enable such souls to live through eternity nearer to Him! He also created His children; every one of them, with potential power and capacity to know Him and to obey Him. He also gave the power of choice to enable everyone to decide to independently investigate to know the Truth of Him, the All-Knowing, the All-Powerful the All-Giver, and the All- Bountiful!

If the generality of people in the body of mankind fail to choose the right and thus refuse to investigate to know who they are and for what purpose they have been created, and instead chose to remain ignorant about the destination awaiting them at the end of their travel in this life, dependent upon whether their soul is developed or not developed and in the end if they reach a level of Hellish conditions and to continue to live an eternal life, deprived of Heavenly conditions, who is to be blamed? Not God! Not anybody but oneself!

Because of the wrong choices made, because of the wrong that has been perpetrated within the body of mankind, at the present moment the world of human beings is in disarray; it is sick and disillusioned!

Do you think a Loving Creator will allow His most cherished children to suffer at the hands of a few selfish, power-crazy, disobedient to the laws of God, always complaining, always grumbling and taking pleasure in killing their own kind to perpetuate power?

Do you think a Loving and an All-Powerful Creator will allow this degenerative disease causing germs that is destroying the body of mankind to perpetuate?

Do you think an All-Powerful and an All-Compassionate Creator will not act when the time is right, to rescue mankind from the mess it has created and existing trapped within?

He will assuredly in His own way rescue this tottering civilization! He has begun to crumple and roll out the Old World Order and have begun to roll in a New World Order in its stead! The world of man is now within the wash that is taking place as these two opposing forces are replacing each other!

New Social Teachings, befitting the advent of a united God-fearing, global civilization, is consciously affecting the thinking pattern of all individuals on this planet! Many feel that a change; the cause of which many are still unaware, is transforming the lifestyles of people everywhere! Those in the know are joining forces to walk the right Highway of life!

During these crucial and critical times when dramatic global cataclysmic changes in the lives of individuals and wholly even on planet earth are taking place; then ask yourself, what role should you play in this drama of life! If you choose to be complacent, someone else will, and you would have lost your opportunity to be part of a glorious future not only on planet earth but also miss an opportunity to live in heavenly conditions throughout eternity!

Read on and try to understand how you too will be able to fulfill the purpose of your creation and be part of this spiritual drama!

Read on and make right decisions.

Read on and be aware of the fact that your future and the nature of that future in the after-life is in your hands!

Chapter 11

The Image Of God In You

You have been created in the image of God. Many have misunderstood this statement and interpreted according to their prejudiced, egoistic understanding! Space does not permit within the confines of this book to go into greater detail to describe the many different statements made and the fallacy of their interpretations.

What does it really mean, when you are told that you are created in the image of God? In order to understand this statement better, it will be of assistance to compare you, the soul with a seed.

If you are told, that the seed is made in the image of the tree, which created it, it means that the likeness of the qualities of the tree is in the seed. In the seed you will know, that latent and potential within it, is the trunk, the branches, the leaves, the flowers and the fruits. The seed has fulfilled the purpose of its creation and lived to fulfill its potentials; the image of its "creator", when it becomes a fruiting tree.

When you know what "image" is in this context, then you will be able to appreciate better, the statement that you are made in the image of your Creator; God!

Image is made up of three factors; the mirror that reflects the image, the light that gives the image life and the image of the thing, that is reflected. When these three factors interact upon each other in synergy, the image is reflected.

In like manner, the image that is created within you is the many qualities of God the Creator. You are the mirror. The Teachings of God sent as the Word of God is the Light and as the result of this interaction between the "mirror" and the "Light"; when you choose to obey and live a lifestyle in obedience to the guidance of God, what you do becomes the image of God in the estimation of the beholder!

The difference between the seed and you as the soul is that, the seed has no choice but to submit to the Will of the Creator! On the other hand, you the soul have the power to make choices, and therefore you can either submit to the Will of your Creator, or choose not to submit! What should be and will be your choice?

When you arrived to be associated with the developing child in the womb-world of the mother you were like a "pure seed" a pure soul!

This soul is the "pure mirror". What is the use of being a pure mirror placed in a dark room? How can it reflect even if the best of the best is placed in front of it? Ask yourself whether this is not the reason; why living without spiritual education, people behave the way they do?

You are created as a perfect "mirror". After you are born and after spending a certain amount of years, you feed your soul with thoughts, words and deeds reflecting ungodly practices, and as a result of which, you are now living in the darkness of ignorance of what is right living. At the same time, the Light of Truth is shining bright, as the noonday sun! Why is this phenomenon so prevalent today? Why has not man taken advantage of this Light? What is "covering" their "eyes"? To know the reason, the cause is very easy! The true answer is..... Prejudice; all kinds of prejudice!

As a human being, do you practice prejudice as a routine, as a habit? Ask yourself! If you do, then beware. You are on the wrong Highway of Life that will NOT lead you to Paradise!

How sad it is, to note that many do not realize that all of us have only One Creator, known by many Names, but all know that He is God. We are all His children, created by the same One True God. Yet, we fight each other with such ferocity; kill and maim each other with such wild fury, something even wild beasts do not indulge in! What has happened to us? When will we think and act sensibly? Do we need more calamities and sufferings to happen, to chastise us; to learn what is right? Wars are waging around the world. Wars provoked by people like you and me! After September 11th, came the war in Iraq; many died. Then came earthquakes; many died. Then came the Tsunami; many more died! What next? How many more calamities have to happen before mankind wakes up? When will mankind know this Truth? When will everyone be prepared to face the Creator with a developed soul? Yet, everyone wants to reach heavenly conditions! Just wanting is not enough for you to get what you want! What then?

Now that you know what you have to do, after understanding the contents this book willingly and lovingly shared with you, you priority choice is to decide to independently investigate Truth by either turning to study the Spiritual and Social Teachings enshrined in Holy Books of the religion you practice, and if it is mentioned therein that the particular Messenger will return once again in a New Name; then pray and beg God to lead you to embrace the Truth! This is the ONLY WAY!

Chapter 12

You Came Into This Dimension Pure And Holy!

As a soul, you arrived to be associated with the growing embryo in your mother's womb. You arrived as a pure, holy soul! You were created in the image of God! Not only you, but also every soul, have all the potential powers and capacities to develop and reflect the qualities and virtues of God!

What happened after that? You began to acquire and empower yourself with virtues or vices of this world.

Look around and you will find that every soul has been created to reflect various ranks or degrees, according to their created capacities, but all came pure and holy!

Though each and everyone were created unique, each with varying capacities to play various roles in the body of mankind, everyone came to live lives that reflected in deeds the guidance of God!

In the body of humankind, each soul has been blessed with a destined role to play in order to be able to be part of a healthy body, and thereby, fulfill the purpose of creation, but along the way, wrong choices were made leading to wrong lifestyles influenced by and aping perhaps their parents, peers and those in authority, and this resulted in such souls to become defiled in their intentions and ways.

Study the human body. Its cells, forms various tissues, organs and appendages, like the limbs, eyes, ears, heart, liver, finger nails, toe nails, hair etc. Each plays a role according to its limitations and capacities, but all participate to serve the whole body! If any one of these fail to perform accordingly, the body tries to heal it, and if it fails to correct the discrepancy, it is rejected and removed from the body itself! Likewise, should you fail to play your destined role, by being disobedient to the Laws and Principles of God; you will be discarded spiritually, because you are not part of the whole! This is justice!

Though you attribute your failure to your parents irresponsibility for not faithfully observing the tenets of God's Faith, nevertheless you cannot be completely forgiven, because you have already been given the power and capacity to play your role in this life effectively, and since you have been blessed to exercise your power of choice; and if you have chosen not to do good but chose to do the wrong, you and you alone have to be responsible for your failure!

Such is God's method in the past and such will it be, forever. Your parents could have assisted you, but that does not absolve you from your failure! Your parents on the other hand will be held responsible for having betrayed the trust of God, by not having nurtured you in the lap of God's Teachings!

The Truth is that you have been lovingly instructed by God, even before you left Him in the spiritual world to be associated with your developing body in the mother's womb. He had told you then, the reason why you are going to travel in this human dimension. He had also clearly informed you, what you are expected to do when you arrive in this human dimension. He also told you what will be the consequence of your failure to obey Him!

You cannot recollect it now, do you? Why? Because the things of this world has dirtied the mirror of your heart; those negative qualities that you have picked up along the way, together with your attachment to this world of illusion; these have clouded your vision! In spite of such loving concern and care by your Creator, you have failed!

Upon the extent of the development of your soul, while you are living and travelling in this life, will depend whether you will be attracted to live eternally in Heavenly conditions or in Hellish conditions. Where you end up in the spiritual world; that responsibility is yours and yours only.

Now you are aware of the Truth about yourself; your SOUL! Will there be any excuse from you should you fail to fulfill this task?

Chapter 13

A Role Play For aA Better Understanding

To enable you to better understand to know God, and the importance of recognizing, accepting and obeying His Prophets and Messengers and Their Teachings, a tool to re-emphasize its importance is in order.

This tool is a role-play. In this play there is a father and his two children. The father is a doctor who owns a very popular clinic and he wants his two children; a boy and a girl, to go to a far off medical university, study, graduate, and then return with medical degrees, to qualify themselves to take over the running of the clinic.

The two children; Jack and Jill are given every facility to enable them to survive the number of years they will spend away from home. The children do not lack anything.

The college term begins and we find that Jill goes to college regularly, follows every instruction in her class and earns recognition as a diligent student. On the other hand Jack becomes playful, does not attend classes regularly, does not study and spends his time with truants like him.

The father sends Jack and Jill, regular letters, in which he renews his pledge of support for his children, repeats the bounty of owning the clinic when they return as doctors, and sharing with them tips, which are his own experiences, whilst he was a medical student. The father expects them to heed his advice. Since both Jack and Jill have the power to make their own choices and make right decisions, the father does not interfere in this matter.

Both Jack and Jill receive these letters but it is only Jill, who reads and re-reads these letters and obeys every instruction from her father. Jack, on the other hand, many a time does not read the letters at all, and even if he has read a few lines and understood the importance of the messages in the letters, he chooses to ignore his father's advice.

Years pass by. Graduation Day arrives. Jill becomes a full-fledged doctor. Jack on the other hand has failed. The time to return has arrived, and both Jack and Jill return home. The father excited about the return of his children, prepare a great feast and invite all those in the town to share his joy.

The children arrive. The father welcomes them both with so much of love and affection! That night the two children are amazed at the grand reception the father had prepared for them. At the end of the day, the father goes up the stage and announces that the clinic will now be taken over by qualified doctors, returned after studying.

The next morning, who do you think becomes the new medical superintendent of the clinic? Jill has taken over. She is a qualified doctor now.

What about Jack? Jack has failed his test. His father gave him the same facilities, advice, love and concern. Yet he failed himself. The reason? He disobeyed his father. He had one golden opportunity to develop himself and he failed. From that moment onwards, Jack will have to remain and live in remorse, because he cannot do anything to reverse time! He becomes a non-entity!

The moral of this story is that obedience to authority guarantees a happy future; obedience to the Laws and Principles of God, guarantee eternal life in Paradise and any form of disobedience will surely guarantee eternal life in the depths of hellish conditions!

In this role-play, the father is (God). The clinic is (Heaven). Jack and Jill are 2 souls. Just as Jack and Jill were given specific instructions by their father about their need to go and get qualifications as a doctor, in order to return to inherit the clinic, in the same way, souls who are sent to be associated with the human body and travel from birth to death, are told by God, why they should obey God, why they should live the right life, why they should acquire spiritual qualities and why they must return to Him to live in Heavenly conditions for evermore!

The soul has been given the power of choice. The soul can either obey the instructions of God, or refuse to obey.

If the soul, obeys God, and in so doing develops spiritual faculties of the soul, it will surely be attracted to live an eternal life in Heavenly conditions.

On the other hand, if the soul disobeys God, how can it be possible for it to develop spiritual faculties; how can it expect to be attracted to live an eternal life in Heavenly conditions? Because it has disobeyed God, it has not developed spiritual faculties and so it can only be attracted towards living an eternal life in Hellish conditions!

It is just like what happened to Jack. Jack who left to go to college to train as a doctor was given advice was given everything he will need from the time he leaves his father to go to a Medical College and until he returns. Jack chose to disobey his father and in the end when the time came for his return, he had failed to develop qualifications of a doctor and in the end, it was not the father but he, Jack himself, who judged his non-capacity and instead of inheriting the clinic (Heavenly condition) he had to settle to be a nobody (Hellish condition) for the rest of his "eternal" life! God does not judge you; you judge yourself!

Chapter 14

The Truth Revealed

You are a soul! You are an immortal being. You have come from God . You are associated with the body. With the body you travel. You travel from birth of the body to death of the body. In this world you have a duty to perform. The duty – to develop your soul. Develop what? – Spiritual faculties or virtues! Undeveloped soul – "dead" soul. Developed soul – "living" soul. Dead soul attracted towards Hellish conditions in the spiritual world. Living soul attracted towards Heavenly conditions in the spiritual worlds. Heaven and Hell are not places. Hell and Heaven describe deprived and acquired state of the soul.. After body dies, soul disassociates. The soul leaves to enter the spiritual world. In the spiritual world, the soul lives eternally. Yours is the choice - where do you want to be living eternally?

When will you come to realize that you are created to arrive in this material world, in this human dimension, to live as a human being, in order to choose to "reflect the image of God", in thoughts, words and deeds?

When will you come to realize that you have been created with all spiritual virtues and which are within you in a potential form? These potential virtues within you will have to be unearthed during this lifetime in order to enable you to release the powers within you, and enable you to live the role that will make you to be a part of an empowering an ever-advancing civilization; a civilization that will reflect, unity of mankind, and thus progressively assist to establish an era of Global Unity, Peace, Prosperity and Happiness of all that dwell on earth!

When will you come to realize that you cannot and will never know, how much more time you have left in this life, to begin to play the role you are destined to play, and if you should miss this precious opportunity; that's it!

God is our Creator. God is also our loving Father. He created you because of His love for you.

You are His child. He will never leave you lost and alone without guidance. He will never burden you beyond your capacity. He created souls and sent these souls to live for a certain period as human beings on planet earth. This He has destined, to enable YOU; the soul, to develop spiritual faculties, so that you will be ready to take over as spiritual entities, for spiritual tasks in the spiritual worlds of God. What is the reward? Living eternally in Paradise! What is the punishment? Living eternally in Hellish conditions!

From the dim recesses of ancient times, humans also populated the earth; souls like you; created by God. Even from those times and in every era, He had sent amongst His children in various parts of the planet, His Prophets and His Messengers, Who were His Ambassadors; and Who have been commissioned to reveal to those living during Their appearance the Teachings; the Guidance of God. This has been an ongoing process from a beginning that has no beginning and will continue until the end that has no end! Such a process has been done to enable His children to know and abide by His Teachings, and to return as a fully developed soul to their spiritual home after fulfilling the purpose why the souls have been created! When these souls reach their spiritual home they live there eternally! According to the quantum of development of developed spiritual faculties, all returning souls are attracted to conditions that are either Heavenly or Hellish!

There should be no doubt in your mind that you will surely, one day in the future, leave this human dimension and enter the spiritual world.

Upon the extent of the development of your soul, while you are living and travelling in this life, will depend whether you will be attracted to live eternally in Heavenly conditions or live eternally in Hellish conditions. To make the right choice and decide to act upon it is your responsibility; yours and yours only. That is why when you receive news of who you are and why you have been created a human being, yours the duty to independently investigate the Truth of this message and in deeds live a life accordingly!

Now you are aware of the Truth about yourself; about your soul! Is there any excuse you can bring to God should you fail to reach Him in Paradise with a virtues-developed soul?

Chapter 15

<u>Travel To Reach Where?</u>

There comes a time when we travel in this human dimension to arrive at a junction. It is at this junction we "see" many roads forking forwards. We will have to choose the right road to travel onwards to reach the right destination.

The choice of the road we decide to continue to travel onwards will depend on where we want to reach! Choosing to travel onwards on the right road will take us to the right destination. Should we choose the wrong road to travel onwards, we will surely reach the wrong destination. There will be no going back in time and space after that! You will reach any one destination and there you will be living through eternity!

Be assured that you will travel in this human dimension only once. Every moment is precious. There is no doubt that you have been destined to read this book by a loving, guiding Creator! There should be no doubt about it. Our Loving Creator will guide you in many ways so that we will be able to choose and make our own decision to walk the Right Highway of Life.

In order to make choices it is important that we must have knowledge about the various scenario from which to choose. Do not doubt at all, because the knowledge of the various scenarios from which to choose have always in every era been transmitted to you as His Teachings through His Chosen Prophets and Messengers. Upon the passing of such Prophets and Messengers, Their Sayings have been recorded in Books which are known as the Holy Book of that Messenger. It is when the people in the know, read, understand, and immerse themselves in faith and belief in that Teachings follow in deeds the guidance given; this then bring about a Religion!

The right road we will want to choose to continue to travel onwards is a road from the junction that we will travel upon to reach at the "Hour of Death"; that spiritual doorway that will enable us to enter either Paradise or Hell and to live where we reach to spend our eternity there!

It is when we travel on this right road; this Right Highway of Life we have been destined to travel, will we be able in the interim; during our travel, to live a life in deeds that will enable us to develop spiritual virtues. It is choosing to life such a life in obedience to the guidance given in the Teachings of God that will bring about a paradigm shift that will lead to the crystalizing of unity in diversity, followed by the establishing of peace amongst the body of humankind leading to prosperity and happiness of all living on planet earth!

(It is the quantum of spiritual virtues that the soul has developed during this human existence which will enable the soul to be attracted to enter either Heavenly conditions or Hellish conditions. This in Itself is a great motivating factor for every human being on earth to life right lifestyles)

Now, as you read this book you are at this junction! Now is the time for you to want to independently investigate what has been revealed to you in this book. Should your heart be moved to accept the Truth that has been lovingly explained in this book, you will want to know more information and more details. The publishers of this book will make it easy for you to reach the author with your questions or suggestions or opinions in order to fortify your resolve to fulfill the purpose for which a Loving Creator has created you.

Do not rest until you are sure that you have been created a human being in this Age to know:

That you are created for a specific purpose

That at a particular time in your life as you travel from birth to death of the body you will reach a junction where a specific message will be given to you.

That after listening and trying to understand the message, you will want to know more and you will begin an independent investigation to want to know whether the message is true or not.

When you realize that after independent investigation that the Message you received is true, you will then know that the purpose for which you are created a human being, is to fulfill a purpose God has purposed for you!:

Be assured that you are created to know God and to serve Him and you are one of the bricks in the foundation being built for the laying of a new civilization that will reflect in the body of mankind, unity, peace, prosperity and happiness. This is destined to happen.

To change the world; first you must change. You have been created with the power and capacity to initiate change within yourself. This change must reflect the will of the Creator. Independently investigate and you will know. Your eternal existence in Paradise depends wholly on what you want to do while you can and while you are still living in this human world. Now that you know that you and only you are responsible for the development of spiritual virtues of your soul have you any excuse?

Be a catalyst to initiate unity of all people In the body of mankind. You can! Pray and you will be guided at all times to do what is right. Remember always that we are here on earth as the builders of a new and progressive civilization and our children and future generations will inherit what we have built!

Be happy and you will be very happy once you discover who your really are and how you can fulfill the purpose for which you have been created in this Day. You will be happy to know that you can be part of the spirit that will animate a New World Order!

Civilization is progressive. Civilization comes and goes and every time a new civilization is established after the former, the All-Knowing

Dr. M.M. Sreenivasan

Creator reveals laws to enable mankind to know, to understand and to establish that new civilization. History reveals to us all exactly this Truth!

Chapter 16

What more can be shared?

To the best of my knowledge, with a sincere wish to share this most vital information to all people in the world I decided to write this book. The information couched within the covers of this book must reach the hearts of every human being on planet earth! This information must be known to all before it is too late.

To want to know who I am, and what am I doing as a human being on planet earth, I have, during more than 50 years of study and research, arrived at an understanding what the Almighty Creator wanted us to know. Before that happened I searched here and there to want to know from where will I get the right information about life itself. If I am a traveler in this life I wanted to know my destination. Many of the answers I discovered I have shared with you in this book. There are many more discoveries which I will relate for your sake in the future. These answers I share with you is as a result of beseeching God's guidance and in return He rewarded me with His inspiration while writing this book!

It is Truth that if religious teachings either in the Holy Books of God, or those interpreted by so-called custodians of God's Teaching, do not synchronize with what science teaches, it is either superstition, idle imaginings or sheer fantasy! I have throughout this book followed this method. You are the judge! Every statement written in the script of this book has been weighed on the scale of science and religion and have been found to be balanced!

From the time we were born into this human world as human beings, we know that with the passage of time, inevitable death of the body will happen. That moment when we depart from this world is a most significant time. It is at this time also known as the "Hour of Death", when the departing soul will know what all it did not know while living as a human being in this human dimension.

The soul did not know how much of spiritual virtues it has developed, although it knows about this exercise. At the Hour of Death, the soul will know how much it had developed spiritually. If the soul leaves this dimension a developed soul it will rejoice! On the other hand if the soul had not developed spiritual virtues and become a deprived soul, it will suffer from "eternal remorse".

Such a tragedy which is as a result of not developing spiritual virtues must never happen to any living human being on planet earth! This is my fondest wish.

Now that I know what every human being should know I have made it my life's mission to reach out to all in the world with this Truth.

Perhaps it might be because of my intense love for all human beings whom I consider as members of one human family living in one home; planet earth, that in writing this book I have many times repeated certain facts, certain Truth again and again under different contexts to assure that such acts and Truth sink deep in their hearts. I had to read during my research some passages again and again many times before Truth revealed itself.

Some who read this book might find it difficult to understand the concepts shared therein. Some might also want to not to know the Truth. Some might not believe what is shared in this book. Some will also find fuel to ridicule certain facts stated therein. Never mind! Every human being is created unique! The dialectic of opposites that prevail in creation causes to motivate to learn what is right and what is wrong; what to choose and what not to choose for that human being who wants to do the right!

This is an Age of justice. Justice will prevail and no one can stop the Will of the Creator. Justice stands on two pillars; reward and punishment! It is the law of God that good attracts rewards and bad attracts punishment. To live an eternal life in Paradise is the reward. To know what to do and despite of that fact to choose to do the wrong will assuredly attract punishment and that will be an eternal life of remorse!

To assist the sincere seeker of Truth, more publications with greater in-depth facts will be shared soon. Suffice it to state that this book is a primer and understanding its contents will motivate the seeker to want to know more.

May you taste "maana" from heaven and inhale the sweet fragrance of His All-Encompassing love!

Chapter 17

Two Events That Teach About Truth

This chapter is written as I was about to finish the last chapter of my book "You Will Not Die" When I watched the newscast that showed the victorious and astounding last moments of a miraculous happening I felt urged to include certain pertinent facts which had been discussed in the earlier chapters of the book.! What I am referring to is about the miraculous rescue of the 33 Chilean miners who were trapped for 69 days and 8 hours, 2000 feet deep down rocky earth.

Going by past history of such events as this, the most that had been done was to attempt to try a rescue the unfortunates trapped deep down inside, and when found that was not possible, nearly always the poor victims were left to die.

In this frightening incident in Chile what was the power that contributed to enable a successful rescue? What was the power that galvanized the people of Chile and their government to rise up against insurmountable obstacles to attempt and finally succeed to rescue all the trapped miners?

Such was the tragic and heart-rending nature of the incident; such was the world-encompassing publicity given to this incident, such was the concern of the people of the world bonding their hearts and their prayers; praying for a successful rescue resulting in the fact that no other event in recent times had attracted the attention of the people of the world since the tragic death of more than 3000 people on September 11th in the Twin Towers in New York.

Could these two events be a harbinger of worse events to come or a clarion call to the people of the world to change? How many in the world would have wanted to know why such an event happened? This article is written to share with the people of the world, what could be the hidden significances behind these two heart-rending and attention-grabbing events!

It will be interesting and also educative to study these two events and try to find out whether there is within it hidden messages for the people; you, me and every human being to know and to choose to change to become better human beings!

When the Twin Towers crashed, more than 3000 innocent human beings helplessly trapped inside these two colossal buildings lost their lives. In the morning of that day they left their homes to pursue whatever duties they had to perform in the many offices in these two buildings. Assuredly, before they left their homes that morning it could have been very possible that they must have made plans with their spouses and their family members and friends, perhaps promising them what they will do once they return that evening!. However, a few hours later after entering the Twin Towers, and a little later, within a few minutes all lost their lives in a horrendous manner. What did this tragic event teach mankind?

This tragic event taught the fact that death will visit any one anytime and anywhere and death which signifies the time of leaving this human dimension, always comes without any warning! There are only two happenings in the life of every human being; happenings over which no one have a choice. These happenings are one, when to enter this human world and two, when to leave this human dimension! Both these happenings are entirely within the power and will of the Creator! The time-frame between the coming in and going out from this material human world has a purpose! What is that purpose? By the time you have reached this chapter and after reading the earlier chapters of this book, the reader would have gained a right perspective of the purpose! The next question to ponder over is: *Is my soul developed and ready with soul-faculties to continue to live in the spiritual world, I am now thrust into, after the death of the body, to live eternally in Heavenly conditions?* This question can be answered only by that particular individual living within all humankind, and who is the only one privy to one's lifestyle; a lifestyle based on choosing to fulfill the purpose of one's life in the human dimension!

When news spread about the tragedy that happened in Chili; news that 33 miners were trapped about 2000 feet deep down the earth in a rocky mine and that going by past such incidents, it would be impossible to rescue them; people around the world stunned by such an event looking at the face of tragedy could only wish some miracle to happen to save the lives of these unfortunate men! In the end the impossible happened and the miners were saved! What did this miraculous event teach mankind?

There is no doubting the fact and the Truth is that if the miners one or all were destined by the Creator to die, no power on earth could have stopped the Will of the Creator from happening! Now we are aware that these trapped miners were not destined to die. What could have been the Plan of God relevant to this incident? Did God want to use this incident to teach the people of the world? We know that God is the greatest Teacher and is the Greatest Educator, Who has sent His curriculum through His Chosen Prophets and Messengers. What was He trying to teach us? Perhaps the answer to this question will wake sleeping souls around the world and enable these souls to know what has to be done in order to fulfill the purpose of their creation in this Age!

Let us compare True education as a chain with many links. If the chain has ten links and each of the links can carry a weight of ten kilograms, the total weight the chain with links can carry is ten kilograms. Now, let us suppose that in a chain with ten links, nine links each of which can carry a weight of ten kilograms but one weak link in the chain can carry only one kilogram. In this case the total weight the chain can carry is only one kilogram! The chain is only strong as its weakest link!

Educating every human being even from the womb of the mother is very important. However it is the nature and the quality of education that can be effective and bring forth human beings that can be considered as those who have lived truly purposeful lives and become the true leaders amongst mankind! These true leaders are those who will lead the flock to achieve unity, peace, prosperity and happiness of the body of mankind.

Has the chain of education that is being instituted all over the world in this Age brought about a loving, noble, caring, and sharing, human society on planet earth? The answer is an emphatic and a resounding NO!

What could be the reason, why we of this generation are building a broken and a diseased human society for our children and future generations to inherit? The example of the weakest link in a chain is the mode to investigate to reach and answer.

Amongst the many modules that are incorporated in the curriculum of teaching all over the world, the weakest or the missing link in this chain is a module that imparts True Spiritual Teachings. This module which is about Truth involves knowledge of the immortal self of a human being, commonly known as the soul.

Since a human being is both a physical and a spiritual being, imparting knowledge of only the physical and the material is why generations after generations are living lop-sided lives! Physical and material education is only to live a life in this material illusory world! True Spiritual Education is what will give "life" and empower the spiritual soul to contribute its nobility to make this world; a world of unity, peace, prosperity and happiness. At the same time these accumulated virtues reflecting the "image" of God, will enable the soul to continue its journey to live eternally in the Spiritual World beyond!

Why is this missing or weak link; a link responsible to teach about one's true self; to teach about one's purpose of living as a human being not included in any educational curriculum? Is it because it is considered not so important? Who has decided that it is not important? Has anyone researched to know why is it, that the prevailing physical and material education which has been in force now and centuries throughout the past, did not achieve to bring about unity, peace and prosperity of the body of mankind?

These two events that mankind will not forget; will never forget, represents two important lessons from the Almighty Creator; One Who created you, me, and every human being on earth! Negligence on the part of any human being to not to independently investigate to know what Our Creator is trying to teach us to enable us to obey His Teachings in this human world, will surely result in the soul of that culprit being relegated to leave this human dimension deprived!

When one attempts to investigate the nature of the two events, it will be clear that, one event is about "death" and the other event about "life". One is about transgressing the Law of God and the other obeying the guidance from God! One leads to remorse and the other to joy! One is darkness, the other Light! This dialectic of opposites set in place is to teach human beings an important aspect of life; why it is important to be educated in the Laws of God within Spiritual Teachings! It is futile and absurd to emphasize and attach greater importance to illusionary material life, while neglecting the true aspect of spiritual life. This negligence which affects millions over millions of human beings will only result in the end to enter the Spiritual World with a soul deprived of spiritual virtues; resulting in that soul being relegated to a hellish condition and to live there eternally! It is frightening to imagine but it is the Truth!

To understand better the above statement it is necessary to know a Truth, that everything that is created by God obeys and must obey a stipulated

Law. For example planet earth is created by the same Almighty Creator and the law governing its function is to go round the orbit of the sun once in 365 and ¼ days. The planet has in obedience through centuries obeyed this law! The planet did not possess a power to disobey its Creator. This is because it is created without the power of choice.

Human beings on the other hand are created with the power of choice. Only human beings can choose to disobey the laws of God! Obedience to the Law of God will result in unity, peace, prosperity and happiness of the people of the world. Disobedience on the other hand will result is disunity, prejudice, poverty suffering and unhappiness for the majority, resulting in killing and warring amongst human beings who have truly been created to reflect in their lives love for each other!

The whole natural universe is in balance because natural laws of God keep everything in its place and nothing in creation can work against the law of the Creator Who designed them and also instinctualized within their role to perfection! Nothing in creation either created by God or human beings can go against the purpose for which they have been created. But amongst all created entities, only the human being can go against the Will of the Creator. Why? Because, only human beings have been created with the power of choice to either obey or disobey the Laws of the Creator! These laws are for the purpose to enable the human souls to know, to obey in deeds and to develop spiritual qualities or virtues. These spiritual qualities are to be developed by the soul during their X number of years of living and travelling in the human dimension. The moment the soul leaves this human existence it can only take with it that much of developed virtues and no more, and this soul will have to live with only that much of spiritual virtues throughout eternity in all the worlds of God! Who is aware of this Truth? Yet it is a Truth every human being must know! Everyone must know this Truth before they leave the womb of this material world. It is frightening to think about, but it is the Truth!

Not understanding this Truth before their X number of years expires will be a mistake. It will be a mistake because no human being can afford to postpone developing the soul with virtues when one can. This is because, no one can foretell when the time will come; when they will have to leave this world. Birth and death is not within our power of choice! Death unheralded can visit us at any time!

The message that mankind must be educated with from the September eleventh tragedy is this; that death comes to human beings at a time when one least expect it! At that time, will the soul be ready with developed virtues to leave this human world and enter into the spiritual world? In the spiritual world there is no power of choice or the means to want to develop the soul further? This inability will be the cause for the undeveloped soul to suffer at the "hour of death" eternal remorse. Such a deprived soul will continue to live and progress; but will progress in that same condition through eternity. If this does not cause the soul to suffer eternal remorse, what else will?

The miraculous saving of the trapped miners is a lesson to teach the world, how unconditional love and unity of thought and purpose, of the people of that nation brought forth a miracle of life! The whole population of Chile in unity prayed beseeching the Almighty Creator to assist in whatever means possible to save the trapped miners from the face of death! The whole population of Chile must have exercised such a loving, sharing and caring unity that would have attracted ideas and the means to device the right technology to save the trapped men! Even the President of Chile upon receiving and embracing the last of the trapped miners said, *"Chile will never be the same again"*

The question is: Is it necessary for any nation to face a dangerous life-threatening calamity before it is brought to its senses? Is it necessary for any nation to be brought to its knees before they learn? Who will suffer if that happens? The people will suffer! Which true God-fearing leader of any nation will allow any human being under one's care and jurisdiction to suffer?

Where there is love and unity nothing is impossible. Let us not search for peace. Let us on the other hand use every strategy to bring people together in unity. Then peace will find its place. Searching for peace before strategizing to bring about unity is like putting the cart before the horse! If that is the mode of strategizing the dawn of peace on planet earth; it will never happen!

The common factor in the make-up of all human beings is the soul. Let the thinkers and leaders of the world study about the soul and impart this knowledge to all on earth. Is there any better way to enthuse the minds of the people of the world to know and realize that there is only One Almighty Creator, One Human Family and One Home for all; planet earth!

Let these two ground-breaking, heart-rending incidents teach a lesson to every human being in every nation. Let leaders and right thinking people everywhere begin to ideate, to create ways and means, to propagate unity amongst the people! It Is possible! Faith and belief in the love and power of the One True God will make it possible for the Light of Unity to illumine the hearts of all! This is the spirit of this Age! But first they must be ready to sacrifice old habit-patterns and lifestyles and then begin to learn to live new lifestyles that will resonate with the Will of the Almighty Creator! With the power of God they will attract when such a resolution enters the hearts of all, the power of God will then descend to make unity, peace, prosperity and happiness of mankind come true!

Let the fear of God be the commander of our lives!

The Will of the Creator is like sunshine. Sunshine does not show any favoritism. It shines on all alike. All are created from the same dust! All are created by one All-Mighty Creator. All must live as members of one human family. And we know that we all live in one home; our planet earth! Why then should we be living in prejudice? Why should differences trap us to cause to hate each other? How long have we, to discard such ignoble practices that has become the cause of disunity and so prevent the dawn of global unity and global peace? How long will it take for any human being to realize that in whatever they do wearing the glass of prejudice, they will assuredly damage their souls?

The horrible conditions prevailing within the body of humankind all over the world in this day are deteriorating with every passing day. We do not have much time to develop our souls to reach a joyous eternal life if we do not wake up to reality NOW! So let us all pledge to ourselves to begin as soon as possible, even now, to independently investigate as to how to walk the right Highway of Life!